FEAR TO GLORY

Be delivered from the spirit of fear!

CHANDRIKA MAELGE

WestBow
PRESS®
A DIVISION OF THOMAS NELSON
& ZONDERVAN

WestBow Press books may be ordered through booksellers or by contacting:

WestBow Press
A Division of Thomas Nelson & Zondervan
1663 Liberty Drive
Bloomington, IN 47403
www.westbowpress.com
844-714-3454

Scripture quotations marked NLT are taken from the Holy Bible, New Living Translation, copyright © 1996, 2004, 2007. Used by permission of Tyndale House Publishers, Inc. Carol Stream, Illinois 60188. All rights reserved.

Scripture quotations marked NKJV are taken from the New King James Version. Copyright © 1982 by Thomas Nelson, Inc. Used by permission. All rights reserved.

ISBN: 979-8-3850-3146-7 (sc)
ISBN: 979-8-3850-3145-0 (e)

Library of Congress Control Number: 2024916704

Print information available on the last page.

WestBow Press rev. date: 11/13/2024

CONTENTS

DISCLAIMER: *The personal testimony is the author's life experience. It reflects the author's present recollections of the experiences over time. Specific names are NOT mentioned in the personal testimony, if a person feels a certain character represents them it is purely coincidental.*

Cover Image: SHINE YOUR LIGHT, is a mixed medium collage art by Chandrika Maelge, from the series Let There Be Light 2018.

Photography: Author's profile image, and ART photography by Kesara Ratnavibhushana and team. All other images by Chandrika Maelge.

DEDICATION

The book is dedicated to all the intercessory prayer warriors, who answered my call for prayers, every step of the way in writing and publishing this book. Thank you for being pillars of love, light, and strength.

In Christ,

Chandrika Maelge

Introduction

4th Dec 2023 was a gloomy rainy day in our beautiful village. The Holy Spirit nudged me to begin writing this new book for the new season. My sofa cum bed was calling me to sleep a bit more, looking at the rain falling on a forest-like garden. Yes, my heart was trying to find an excuse. Yet, my spirit, strengthened by the Holy Spirit connected me to my spiritual prayer partner. We prayed in the early hours and submitted the book project to the leading of the Holy Spirit, according to God's will.

We submitted it all to the Lord!

To write one must have a good space. With the COVID lockdown, I had neglected two of my rooms. I had moved into the living room. I was making plans to give a facelift to these two rooms and then begin writing the book. However, it appears that my plans are not His plans. So, I created a writer's space in the TV lounge area with a wide-open space to the garden. The coffee table became the writer's table. The lounge chair became the writer's chair.

Surrounded by art titled WORD OF GOD, HARVEST, and GLORY; I began to write this book.

I told myself, "C, *keep away from social media. It is the Christmas season. So many temptations. So many distractions.*" I was determined to finish writing the book, despite the many challenges. In the process of writing this book my life went through a personal transformation. Often, I was led to deeper levels of prayer, waiting on the Lord to begin writing. Writing the book was a secret known only amongst the few prayer intercessors and my mother, up until the later stages.

At the start with great drive and passion, I wrote the manuscript in about two months. Then the Holy Spirit led me on an intense period of prayer, repentance, forgiveness, and healing. A time of writer's block, where I could not write until I had dealt with unforgiveness and begun to genuinely pray for those who had hurt me. In this period, I received many instructions from the Lord, through prayer, to edit many words in the manuscript.

This is a story of deliverance from the spirit of fear.

In this testimony, I have highlighted many mistakes I made over the years, which allowed great fear to enter my mind and attack me. I share my heart and vulnerabilities, with the hope of helping brothers and sisters in Christ not to repeat such mistakes, which can even derail one's journey in faith. I write led by the Holy Spirit, to glorify God and encourage others.

OBJECTIVE OF THE BOOK

The objective of the book is to encourage Christians; to overcome and triumph over the spirit of fear, arise in the light of the word of God, and shine bright in His glory.

I have set the stage for the testimony by emphasizing a Holy Bible story where fear was able to grip Elijah the prophet of the LORD.

In relation to the testimony; the WORDS OF ENCOURAGEMENT chapter highlights three important areas a Christian can embrace in the journey of faith, especially in overcoming fear. Holy Bible stories and scripture references are made where applicable, in supporting the narrative.

Share this book. Be builders of faith and encourage fellow Christians. For nonbelievers, may this book plant words of light in your hearts.

It is purely God's grace, goodness, and strength that enabled me to write this book. I am grateful!

Be delivered from the spirit of fear
.... (Insert your name in the space), in Jesus Christ the Lord's name. Amen.

FEAR

Have you ever choked on fear? Well, I have. Fear gripped me so tight that I could not breathe. I nearly lost all my faith. I said, I nearly lost all faith. I could not even pray!

Fear oppresses, torments, and terrorizes one's mind.

As long as you are under the thumb of fear, you are not free. Fear will keep you imprisoned and immobilized and prevent you from living the life God intended you to live. Fear can only attack you if you give it access. At a time when I was weak, exhausted, and very vulnerable, my actions, and especially; the doors I opened, gave access to the spirit of fear to enter and create great chaos in the mind. I was caught off-guard!

It was the greatest test of faith I had faced.

In the Holy Bible, we come across many occasions where fear gripped God's people, even servants of God. I have chosen to highlight, the story of Elijah the prophet of the LORD, and the Mount Carmel prophet challenge along with events that took place thereafter, to set the stage to share my testimony.

MOUNT CARMEL PROPHET CHALLENGE

Elijah announces at Mount Carmel, that he is the only prophet of the LORD left, and Baal has 450 prophets (1 Kings 18:22).

1 Kings 18: 23 to 24 explains the challenge presented by Elijah. Each side was to prepare their altar and place the sacrifice of the cut pieces of the bull on the wood, and no one was allowed to light the wood. Each side was to call upon their deity by name, and the deity that answered the call of their prophet by setting fire to the wood would be the true God of Israel.

Elijah told the prophets of Baal to prepare the bull for the sacrifice first and asked that they refrain from setting fire to wood and call on their god (1 Kings 18:25).

1 Kings 18: 26-29, explains how Baal's prophets faced this challenge. Baal's prophets prepared their altar with the bull sacrifice. They called upon Baal from morning till noon. There was no answer. Then Elijah mocked the prophets of Baal. Then these prophets of Baal screamed and cried, they cut themselves to the point that blood poured out of them. Baal's prophets prophesied until evening. Still, there was no sound heard.

No answer was given.

1 Kings 18:30-35, explains how Elijah prepared his altar. Elijah got the people to come over and inspect as he repaired the LORD's altar, which was broken down. He took 12 stones, to represent the tribes of the sons of Jacob, whom the LORD named Israel, and built an altar in the LORD's name. He dug a trench around his altar. He piled the wood in the middle and placed the cut pieces of the bull sacrifice on the wood. Elijah got the people to fill large water jars and pour the water on the wood and the cut pieces of the bull. Three times, he drenched the offering with water. Water filled the trench.

As per 1 Kings 18:36, the prophet Elijah prayed to the LORD, God of Abraham, Isaac, and Jacob at the time of the evening sacrifice. Elijah requested that; the LORD prove to all that He is the God in Israel, and he, Elijah is indeed a servant of God and has done all these things as per God's command.

In a flash, the fire of the LORD came down from heaven and burned up all things on Elijah's altar. Even the water in the trench was no more (1 Kings 18:38).

There was an answer given to prophet Elijah's prayer request! Fire from above.

Thereafter, on Elijah's command, people caught all prophets of Baal. Elijah took these prophets of Baal to Kishon Valley and killed them (1 Kings 18:40).

In 1 Kings 17:1; Elijah proclaimed a drought of many years to King Ahab. In 1 Kings 18:41 Elijah informs Ahab that a storm is coming. Thereby, announcing the end of the drought.

Having said this,

ELIJAH THE LORD'S PROPHET PUT HIS FACE BETWEEN HIS KNEES AND BEGAN TO PRAY. ELIJAH **PRAYED 7 TIMES** ON TOP OF MOUNT CARMEL. AND IT RAINED HEAVILY!

(1 Kings 18:42,44,45)

ELIJAH RAN IN FEAR

King Ahab went and told Queen Jezebel, what Elijah had done and how Elijah had killed all Baal's prophets (1 Kings 19:1). Then Jezebel sent a message of threat to Elijah, that she would kill him by this time tomorrow (1 Kings 19:2).

Take note, that it was a message of threat that was sent.

When Elijah received this threatening message, fear gripped him, and he ran in fear for his life. Having left his servant at Beersheba, Elijah traveled a day's journey to the wilderness sat under a tree, and prayed to the LORD that he might die (1 Kings 19: 3,4).

It seems Elijah was overwhelmed.

This mighty prophet Elijah, who performed great signs and wonders and single-handedly killed all of Baal's prophets, became so afraid of the threatening message sent by a woman named Queen Jezebel.

Words are powerful. Words can cause fear!

Elijah was victorious at the Mount Carmel prophet challenge. Yet, in that moment of fear, Elijah prayed that he might die.

#

Dear Reader,

As per this story, we
see that it was,

WORDS OF THREAT

THAT

FRIGHTENED ELIJAH!

AND HAD HIM RUNNING IN
FEAR FOR HIS LIFE!

A man, a mighty and bold prophet of
the LORD, becomes fearful and afraid
just because of words of threat.

WORDS ARE POWERFUL!

#

You may be a mighty apostle, prophet, evangelist, teacher, or pastor, I urge you to watch out for the attack by the spirit of fear. All things you have done to glorify God in the past are irrelevant at that moment. Faith goes down almost to zero! Fear can choke out the very confidence one has in God. Fear can strangle you like a giant python.

In my moment of fear, I did ask God to take me away, take me away from this place. 'THIS PLACE'; I am referring to is my home.

In that moment of fear, I forgot the promises of God. This house is a gift of inheritance. The house went through major renovations in 2009. All interiors were completely changed. This is where I discovered the passion to make new the old. From 2017 to date, this place became my sanctuary to '*DO THINGS IN SILENCE*' as instructed by God. It was from here that the art and words ministry began. It was from here that I went on my first overseas mission. It is a place of spontaneous worship and prayer. I recorded my first teachings on BRAND NEW YOU IN CHRIST and the GOOD NEWS from this place. It is my art studio, recording space, and writer's space. It is my place with the Holy Spirit. My sanctuary, by way of deceptive words, turned into a place of terror.

Now, let me share my testimony.

PERSONAL TESTIMONY

In late November 2023, I was physically and emotionally exhausted. Various trials and simply life had brought me to a stage of burnout. It was at a time like this, that my garden pots and statues were stolen. This trivial incident spiraled its way out of control leading to the greatest test of faith I faced in my life.

I enjoy gardening.

The garden is almost a forest, home to a troop of purple-faced leaf monkeys, porcupines, mongooses, civet cats, and many other small mammals. Nearly a hundred species of birds including; a few winter rarities, two owl species, and eagles, make this garden their home. The garden is also home to the not-too-pleasant scorpions, snakes, vipers, water monitors, and land monitors. Amidst the giant trees, a lush green lawn, and an array of flowers are giant pots and statues. It was these pots and statues that were stolen. I went to lodge a complaint at the police station.

Now normally, I would have surrendered all things to the Lord asking for words and wisdom seeking His grace, and moving ahead as an Ambassador of Christ.

This time around; I simply went to meet a new religious counselor.

Those who have followed my journey in faith would say I do things in RADICAL FAITH. From the onset, a relationship with God was the most important relationship I treasured. When I am nudged by the Holy Spirit, to do an art exhibition, go on a creative brand assignment, write a book, give, or simply pray at a location; I moved like the wind in the last 10 years. There was great freedom and confidence in my Lord Jesus Christ.

The woman who did two Christian faith-based art exhibitions in Sri Lanka; namely *'JOURNEY OF FAITH: RESPONDING TO GOD'S CALLING'* 2017, *'LET THERE BE LIGHT'* 2018, and wrote a book *'BRAND NEW YOU IN CHRIST'* because she was convinced in her heart regarding what she saw in the Spirit, and the word received during prayers; strangely was now seeking permission from new religious counselors concerning matters of life.

In the past I took decisions as led by the Holy Spirit, presenting the case to the Lord in prayer. Somehow, I did not do what was naturally normal to me.

MISTAKE:

I did not pray and present my burden to the Lord as I used to do in the past. Instead, I simply sought man's advice....

Unfortunately, a new habit has replaced the old. I was slowly beginning to rely more on man.

WHAT HAPPENED?

To dive deeper we need to go back in history. There were many mistakes I made over the years, which had a ripple effect on my journey in faith. These mistakes altered parts of my God-given personality.

UNKNOWN TO ME, I CHANGED.

#

I OPENED A DOOR FOR FEAR

In 2013, I left Sri Lanka as a Buddhist, and I returned in 2015 as a Christian with great faith in Jesus Christ the Lord. I was the only Christian at home.

Now, I began to probe into my roots. My great-grandfather, together with his siblings, came from the south and settled down in the village, where we currently reside. They were Christians. My great-grandfather was a musician, an English teacher, and the principal of his school. He fell in love with a dark tall woman from the village. She was a Buddhist. My grandfather was their eldest son. My great-grandfather died young. So, my grandfather left school to become a farmer.

Stories of the land and its settlers fascinated me.

Some said that my great-grandmother was devoted to astrology, visited shamans, and acted on vows. Well, when I was a Buddhist; I too went to see the astrologers, did what the monk requested, and wore many colors of threads around my wrist. It was family culture. No one questioned it, we just followed after our parents. I remember the many 'Thovil' festivals held in our land, which I watched with great wonder as a child. These rituals and festivals influenced art in my early childhood.

At the back of my mind, I began to feel uneasy about the stories of vows and other stuff practiced by my maternal great-grandmother. There was a sense of uneasiness. Then, I began to notice the many shamans around my residence.

I began to worry and became afraid of witchcraft, dark magic, curses, and spells.

At the time, my mind was worrying about curses and spells; a religious leader singled me out at a large gathering and announced that generational curses must be broken in my life. Having read Exodus 20:5 and Exodus 34:7, I personalized generational curses. I began to worry whether my great-grandfather left his Christian faith. I was the last of the fourth generation. Somehow, I had lost sight of the truth. The truth is, as per Galatians 3:13, I had been redeemed by Christ Jesus from curses mentioned in the law. In addition, I have the delegated authority from Jesus Christ over all the power of the enemy as per Luke 10:19.

The truth was hidden, and the light went out! With it, a door to fear was opened!

On and off, I would dream of a dark tall woman and be terrified. I would wake up sweating. I found it difficult to breathe. In the dream, I would try to speak, yet no words came out. I was choking and gasping for breath. I was terrified and paralyzed with fear.

Night terrors slowly crept in again!

I acknowledged Lord Jesus Christ as my Lord and Savior in 2013 in the Fiji Islands. The first spiritual attacks started almost immediately, in the form of night terrors. I was tormented by night terrors. Dark figures, giant serpents, and sinister laughter terrorized my nights. I used to keep a few lights on and go to sleep afraid.

I went and told all of this to my church pastors in Fiji. The pastors of my local church visited my home. The group prayed boldly. They asked me to stand in my identity as a CHILD OF GOD, take authority, and pray. They assured me, the night terrors would stop. I put faith into action and the night terrors ceased in Fiji. Then I began to live out the brand new life in Christ Jesus in the marketplace.

I came back home to Sri Lanka in 2015. I joined a church. Immediately, I got busy focusing on work in both ministry and the marketplace.

Unfortunately, I failed to mention the 'night terrors' to my pastors in Sri Lanka. I did not think of it to be that serious. Especially, since it did cease in Fiji. I was about to find out how it would come back to haunt me.

MISTAKE:

Failing to address issues (e.g., night terrors) at the start is a recipe for disaster.

A MIND FULL OF WORRY

Life went by, I was kept busy with various art, work, prayer, and mission assignments, so much so that I had no time to think of witchcraft and weird practices that had supposedly taken place in the land many moons back.

Then the COVID lockdown came and introduced a new normal.

I loved going to church. This was where I had fellowship with fellow believers. I loved cooperate worship. The WORD preached always edified me to triumph that week. Sunday was my favorite day! With the lockdown, churches began meeting online. The gathering of saints was not the same. Slowly but surely; I began to watch online church services in my own time. Unknown to me, I was slowly getting distant from my spiritual family.

Those days going on holidays was a luxury. Therefore, I prioritized personal holidays, at any given opportunity. Going to church online was neglected. I began spending more of my time with nonbelievers on holidays and leisure. To add to this; a difference of opinion separated a close Christian friend. Finally, when church resumed meeting physically, the world had distanced me from church!

MISTAKE:

The gathering of the saints was neglected, and personal enjoyment was prioritized.

I was eager to serve in the church. My zeal was met with a questionable eye by most Christians. Someone said I should find my people and start my cell group. Some shut doors to partner with prayer. Unfortunately, I saw all these as rejections.

I allowed these words to enter and pierce my heart. I was easily offended. To avoid getting hurt, I slowly began distancing myself from people and the church. To make matters worse, I left it as it is. I internalized my pain and hurt.

MISTAKE:

I allowed words to enter my heart and create great hurt.

In my hurt, I had forgotten that God had already birthed a ministry of art and words in 2017. I only had to look back and see how God's favor was evidently seen in the assignments done in the past. What was required was to wait, trusting God. Hurt and misunderstood, I left the church and drifted from one place to another trying to fit in. A square peg trying to compromise to fit into a round hole. I was miserable! Harboring thoughts of rejection, my wounded heart got festered.

MISTAKE:

I left the church.

It seemed that if I was not part of a church, I simply did not have Christian friends. Literally, I had two sisters in Christ who connected with me. I missed not having Christian fellowship. I was very lonely. Separation anxiety and worry of isolation entered my mind. I wondered, *"Doesn't anyone care? Am I so unlikable?"*

> *I was about to find out the hard way the consequences of being an isolated Christian.*

As a result of the COVID lockdown, I lost my marketing consultancy projects. To add to it, I was settling into a homebound life brought about, by the lack of job opportunities and the demand at home of an aging parent. A year or two down the line, with more non-working days than working days, I began to worry about my career and depleting finances.

I must mention that I was reading the Holy Bible, spending time with the Holy Spirit, interceding for others, and doing the odd work assignment at that time. My prayer life had moved to focus on the country, church, and spiritual warfare. Yet, inside of me, weeds were growing.

Over time these weeds had grown into big trees!

WHAT WERE THESE WEEDS?

- Fear of witchcraft, dark magic, curses and demons.
- Worry of career stagnation.
- Worry about depleting finances.
- Separation anxiety, and worry of isolation.

ALONG WITH THE WEEDS 'THE TRUTH' WAS GROWING.

- Fed by the Word of God.
- Led by the Holy Spirit.
- Strengthened by prayer.
- Edified by the prophetic.
- Built by the knowledge of Lord Jesus Christ.

#

A PRISONER WAS SET FREE

Let us get back to the little robbery.

Following up on my complaint, the police came to inspect the garden. Having seen the police visiting our home, a villager called and informed us they saw who stole the pots and statues. A day or two later, I was informed that the person who stole my pots and statues was caught, and most items were retrieved.

By this time, I was well-rested and calm.

During morning prayers, I was led by the words *"Go visit the robber in prison."* I went. This time I submitted it all to the Lord! I spoke to the prisoner where he was held temporarily. The Holy Spirit gave me words of wisdom, love, mercy, and correction. Nothing scripted. A simple request was made *"When you are set free, come to church."* Then one asked for prayers. It was a beautiful sunny day. The prisoner was set free to unite with his young family that evening.

I returned home, and joyfully closed the chapter on the little robbery, thanking God. The pots and statues that were recovered made their way home to a newly arranged garden, blooming in beauty. Mercy and love triumphed! Praise God! I was joyful!

ONSLAUGHT ON THE MIND

As do with most people, I too have had my run-in with antagonistic people. They tend to oppress and stress out your mind. Their spoken words are like a hammer pounding on the listener's head.

As I matured in Christ Jesus and began to live out the Christian faith, things took a drastic turn.

The first thing to drop off was my previous social clubbing/pubbing life. At times I had to meet people at pubs, as it was their preferred place of meet-up. Some of these meetings presented an opportunity to witness about Lord Jesus Christ. People would flock around to listen. Then my companions began to say, *"You are not fun anymore, you talk too much of Christ, I don't want to meet you again."* With this, an army of voices arose against me. They had a questionable view of my faith and my life in Christ Jesus, and were very concerned that I was slipping away from the 'things of the world', and was losing touch with how the 'world functions'. Some began to influence others, to advise me to stop living out my Christian faith and stop sharing my faith. As time passed, my opposers became very irritated. They began to voice out and act out their displeasure.

I have been openly rebuked and mocked for my faith in Christ Jesus. The intensity of such mocking increased with time.

Thus, began a life of persecution for being in Christ Jesus.

The attacks started small with reports of lies taken to my superiors for disciplinary action. I could have lost my job. Lord's grace helped me to overcome the trial (2 Corinthians 12:9). Then, it graduated to emails of lies mixed with truth. They threatened letters of complaints will reach my pastors. I showed these emails to my pastors. They made me aware that the enemy can attack the child of God. They requested that I forgive and pray for my accusers. Having read Ephesians 6:12, I understood there is a very real spiritual battle. We are not fighting things of flesh! So really, we are not to fight head-on with the person but engage in spiritual warfare.

Sometimes people are antagonistic, because it's in their nature, an evil spirit is working through them, or a mix of both. I have endured great hardships, unpleasant words, and name-calling, which is shocking to mention. I had forgiven, prayed, done good, and prayed with others. I also prayed for endurance and self-control for myself.

Yet, the attacks did not cease.

I RAN IN FEAR

I had just shut the chapter on the little robbery of pots and statues. Overwhelmed, yet joyful about the outcome, I began to relax. I was alone. It was a tough period in my life, I had no job and most of my old friends had left me! The episode of the little robbery stretched me, physically and mentally. Numerous travels, answering millions of phone calls, and balancing the home front ensuring everyone was safe; added to the already pressurized mind. Physically, I was exhausted. I just wanted to sleep.

Suddenly, the enemy began an onslaught on my tired, exhausted, and overwhelmed mind.

I was caught off-guard. There was no recovery time, no time to pray. The enemy had carefully laid out a trap of deception.

It was a word attack!

Words of lies were mixed with truth and used to frighten me. With God's grace, I had overcome many unpleasant attacks of the enemy in the past; and my mind went into auto-pilot mode.

I was thinking out loud; *"What is the hidden agenda?"*

This time a very strong network of tormenting, oppressing, and deceptive spirits were working together to create great terror in my mind. I felt like a deer caught in a hunter's trap. Something inside of me anticipated great danger to my life. I feared for my life.

Trapped and with no way to go, I felt threatened.

Up until that moment when I faced persecution in the past, I would go pray and declare Isaiah 54:17 with great boldness saying, *"All weapons will not succeed against me. Every tongue that rises against me I will condemn. My vindication comes from the LORD"*. I would proclaim the word and move forward in peace.

Yet, on that day my heart started racing, and my mind was locked up. I was afraid to speak. My mind went into a total block. I could not even think out Isaiah 54:17.

I got emotional. These evil spirits had increased fear in me. Normally, I would have contacted my support group of wise brothers and sisters in Christ. Instead, in my despair, I ran to see a new religious counselor. I turned to new religious counselors who knew very little of my journey in faith. There was a couple.

MISTAKE:

I listened and reacted in fear to the spoken words.

It did not occur to me that these counselors were looking at me with a fresh set of eyes. They barely knew me. On that day, my behavior may have looked like a person with zero faith, with little or no endurance. Whereas, I was an injured deer looking for a sanctuary. I was desperate. I just wanted to pour out my heart to someone.

I hugged the lady and cried.

These new religious counselors requested, that I come in for spiritual counseling. I agreed. I was deeply hurt and frightened; I wanted to talk about the raging storm within me.

MISTAKE:

I opened a door for new and relatively unknown religious counselors to speak into my life.

I prepared for the meeting, in prayer and study of the word. I submitted the meeting to the Lord, took my journals and files, and went to meet these counselors. As I entered, I was asked to keep quiet, and only listen to what was spoken. For saving my soul is their responsibility. He was listening to an online meeting while talking to me. In the end, he had a look at my files, journals, and press cuttings of the exhibitions. They wanted to visit my home. A date was set. At the end of the meeting, I asked if I could worship and leave. My request was granted.

I BEGAN TO WORSHIP.

I began to sing songs birthed by the Holy Spirit in Sinhala, English, and Spirit.

The key shout-out was COME TO THE THRONE OF GRACE!

COME TO THE THRONE OF GRACE!
COME TO THE THRONE OF GRACE! RECEIVE FROM MY GOD!
HE'S THE ONE WHO LIFT UP FALLEN LIVES
HE'S THE ONE WHO HEAL THE BROKEN HEARTS
HE'S THE ONE WHO SET THE CAPTIVES FREE
HE'S THE ONE WHO SET THE PRISONERS FREE
COME TO THE THRONE OF GRACE! RECEIVE FROM MY GOD!
OH... COME AND MEET JESUS CHRIST TODAY.

I closed my eyes and joyfully began singing praises to God. I broke out in tongues. I prayed whilst worshiping. I felt so free and joyful. Almost child-like.

There was no one to witness me dancing and singing.

The hall was empty. Anyway, it did not matter if anyone was watching, I just wanted to worship my God with absolute joy. As I finished my worship and prayers, I could see that it had started to rain heavily. I left the premises with joy in my heart. Singing in the rain!

That evening it rained so heavily that it created a heavy rainwater run-off that looked like a flood.

A VERY STRANGE VISIT

The religious counselors were expected in a few days. It was a rushed visit. I labored a good few days, cleaning, rearranging, and decorating the house preparing it for their visit.

The couple told me not to tell anyone about their visit.

They said they were coming to pray. Being obedient to the request, I told no one. I knew very little about them, yet, as they were religious counselors, I simply trusted them. I prepared my best dish and waited for them to visit.

They arrived at the gate and asked permission to enter.

They said, *"We came, do you give us permission to enter?"* I said, *"Come in! I have opened the gates wide open."* I ushered them into the land. They stepped out of the vehicle and looked around with a puzzled look. They asked permission to enter the house. I said, *"Come in."* I gave them a hug and a kiss. I was happy that they came.

MISTAKE:

In ignorance and haste, I gave permission to access my home, to people I barely knew.

DEAR READER,

HAVE A GOOD LOOK AT THE
COLLAGE ART GIVEN BELOW.

\#

LET THERE BE LIGHT IN YOUR THINKING (2018), collage art gives a pictorial representation of my mind on the day the religious counselors visited me.

The original art is an explosion of color. This is a black-and-white print, so let me explain. Notice the flame of light in the middle of the art. The candle flame has three colors, outer orange, middle gold, and inner yellow. The surrounding area represents the mind I had before Christ. Mind full of worries, uncertainty, fear, doubts, and chaos. The candle flame represents the light of the knowledge of, the Lord Jesus Christ. Notice, that the letters of the words, FEAR and WORRY in the art, are burned out by the candle flame. The art aims to communicate that however chaotic a mind may be, when that mind shifts focus to the word of God, it brings light to the worrisome, fearsome, and doubtful situation. We arise and shine in that light.

MISTAKE:

I did not focus on the word of God, on that day.

There was a storm raging inside of my mind. My mind was overwhelmed. Physically, I was exhausted. The sudden attack by the enemy had already bruised my confidence. I simply put all my hope in these religious counselors. I trusted them.

I did not even open the Holy Bible!

Going forward, I will refer to these new religious counselors as 'visitors'.

They knew that I was exhausted, hurt, and bruised; as I had shared all the details of life's challenges with them. They knew that we were all women, living alone in a forested land. They entered my home and decided to sit in the TV lounge. They were aware of a vision that I had shared with them, about Lord Jesus Christ and the TV lounge area. They wanted to speak to me alone. I obeyed. I trusted them. I was like an injured deer, waiting to receive some water from these 'visitors'.

MISTAKE:

Forgetting sound counsel in the past, not to share details of dreams, visions, and encounters with God; I shared it, with people I barely knew.

The man began to show facial expressions of sensing the atmosphere. Then suddenly, he started talking about the atmosphere being full of sexual sin. Such as; sexual desires, thoughts, and sinful lust of the flesh. He mentioned child molestation, rape, and abuse that had supposedly taken place in the house. He began to question my knowledge, prompting an answer. He asked me, *"Did a girl get raped here? Was a girl sexually molested in this place?"* I was astonished. My expression was completely blank.

#

DISCERNMENT of spirits is a gift of the Holy Spirit (1 Corinthians 12:10). I believe the responsibility of delivering words of discernment rests with the person operating in the gift of discernment. There had been times; when I too had felt great darkness at certain places. Over the last decade, the Holy Spirit has trained me to be refined in the use of words. Yes, there is the sensing of spirits, now what does one do with the information?

ONE CAN CHOOSE TO SPEAK WORDS THAT BUILD FAITH AND STRENGTHEN THE BELIEVER.

#

The two began their conversation.

One was asking questions and the other answered. The woman was very submissive and obedient to the man. I have shown hospitality to religious leaders in the past. This was the first time; I was made to feel very uneasy in my own home. They knew I was hurt and vulnerable, as I had shared all the pain with them. They spoke all sorts of ugly, undesirable, horrid words concerning my home, which added to the already pressurized mind.

The atmosphere started to shift, as a result of all the unpleasant chatter!

They went back to talking about sexual sin in detail. Apparently, much sexual sin was committed in the TV Lounge area.

Thank God for the Spirit of wisdom that spoke through me and said, "*This area was my parent's room …. I renovated it as the TV lounge, and as for child molestation, rape… Those things did not happen here*".

Hearing this, they asked me not to speak. They said they had come to speak. Since I respected them, and honored them, I obeyed. After all, they were religious counselors.

I obeyed the request by the 'visitors', and stopped talking.

In 2013 during a very confused, lost, and broken period in my life, I saw a vision of the Lord Jesus Christ in a blinding light. This prompted me to flip open the Holy Bible, which was gifted to me. The words in 2 Timothy 2:22, just screamed at me, to let go of the lifestyle I was living at that moment. It was a sharp stab at my stomach. I was indeed living in sin and drowning in lust of the flesh. I felt repulsive of my sinful life. To add to this, I received a prophetic word that encouraged me to take an overseas work assignment. I leaped in faith trusting God and left Sri Lanka. It was during this work assignment, that I acknowledged Lord Jesus Christ as my Lord and Savior. With it, the wanting to gratify sexual desires just vanished.

THE FIRST STRONGHOLD, I WAS SET FREE WAS DELIVERANCE FROM SEXUAL SIN.

#

Through, the Spirit of wisdom; I knew these 'visitors' were trying to get me to talk of my past sexual sins. I was confident my Lord Jesus Christ had set me free from sexual strongholds. I testify here, from the moment I left for Fiji in 2013, to to-date as I write these words, I say with joy praising God that I have not had sexual relations with a partner.

Now they changed their conversation to a different angle.

The 'visitors' asked permission to visit my bedroom. The woman entered, had a walk around, and came back with a bad report to the man. Now he wanted permission to visit the bedroom. I informed them, that I had made plans to renovate this room, and an advance was already made. They began to advise me to polish the furniture, get rid of the mattress, and paint the room. To which I said, *"Plans are confirmed, the room won't look the same, and things are changing"*.

Then they saw the graffiti wall art of *JOURNEY OF FAITH*. This is my artistic masterpiece at home which began in 2015 and kept improving for years. My friends love it!

The 'visitors' said, "COVER IT UP!"

I thought to myself, *"Why would artists cover up the work of their hands?"* This room is my art studio, and my place of fellowship with the Holy Spirit.

My home has large windows on both sides. To cut out the harsh bright morning and evening light, I maintain wide-spread tree canopies around the house. These trees provide a good shade to my home. They kept saying no light, very dark. The ceiling is of a dark wood color, which absorbs light. Naturally, it's a cool and well-shaded place.

Now, I was hoping these 'visitors' would enter the one room that I found challenging. This room was cluttered and unclean. It was a room full of broken electrical items, barbwires, old luggage, old broken furniture, rotting cupboards, and other junk. I voiced my concerns about this room to them. They did not even open the door!

They informed me that, they will visit on another day.

The 'visitors' took permission from my mother to enter her room. My mother welcomed them. She is in her late eighties. They requested me to stay away. I stood at the door. They laid hands on her and uttered words.

I was concerned.

Thereafter, the 'visitors' came back to the TV lounge area and requested, that I bring all I had prepared for them. I packed up my favorite dish and as for drinks I said, "*I will give you water*". As I uttered these words, they both went comically wide-eyed and looked at each other, in surprise.

It had slipped my mind that these people had made it a habit to pray on water bottles and give to people. This had become a ritualistic practice. I was made aware they ritualistically pray over their drinking water.

I gave them DETOX water.

The 'visitors' wanted to know my plans for 2024.

Usually, I would willingly share my plans and thoughts with those who are my spiritual mentors. This time, I felt pressured, also I had not made big plans for 2024. I had nothing solid to share with them. It was November. Plans can change as led by the Holy Spirit. Then, I noticed at that moment; that my journal was opened to the page where the Holy Spirit had instructed me to visit a certain religious leader. I cannot recall keeping the journal open.

Suddenly, the visitors asked which home my ex-husband left me. No woman likes to talk about old painful wounds. Wounds, that Jesus Christ the Lord had healed. It was a closed chapter. This made me very uncomfortable. It was this house. So, I said; *"This one."*

They began muttering; *"Men can't stay here, men can't stay here."*

In the course of conversation, they took out of my mouth all sorts of details, concerning the land.

Then they looked at me with stern faces and said;

"Sell this house. Buy a new one. Don't write to your nephews. Men cannot live here. All will be ok. When you leave this place."

I thought to myself; what do you mean men can't live here? My father lived and died here, and so did my grandfather. At that moment, I recalled, they said they came to pray. What is going on here?

I did not respond to their suggestion.

My mind went to auto-rewind. I stopped to think. I recalled, that in our previous meeting, they advised me to name the house for ministry. However, when they visited the house, all their previous advice changed. Now they wanted me to leave my home. Hope was given and hope was snatched! These *'visitors'* knew; that I was committed to giving a 10% of the increase. How much will this land sell? That seems to be the question.

In recent years in the absence of a church and spiritual mentorship, I fell into what looked like an unfruitful season in the eyes of the world. I praise God! I was never in debt, nor did I or my family in Sri Lanka fall ill due to the COVID-19 virus. I thank God for providing my needs and keeping us safe! This is my home. I felt safe here up until this visit.

Then they said,

"Not sure if I should say this ...Hmmm...

THERE IS SOMEONE WIPING BLOOD OFF THEIR HANDS.... CLOSE TO YOU...."

They knew from my expression that I was frightened. That fear had gripped me.

They left the house saying there was a little bit of purple. They described the dark spirits and left.

I WAS TERRIFIED! MY MIND BEGAN TO RUN ITS OWN RACE!

The person with blood in their hands was the trigger....

All fear of practices of magic and stuff that had supposedly taken place in the land, spells, and witchcraft of shamans, and the frightful dark figure of night terror rushed in at lightning speed. I was very afraid and began to panic!

My mind began racing! I could hear my heartbeat! The spirit of fear had gripped me....

I texted these religious counselors mentioned that I needed counseling, and added that what they said frightened me.

I could not find words to pray at that moment.

Thank God for the *'little faith'*, that sprang into action! I called a sister in Christ and a brother in Christ. They were put on speaker mode. They prayed. Their words echoed in the house. One rebuked the dark forces. Almost an hour later my faith was built, and I began to act on faith.

With my brothers and sisters in Christ praying for me, I began to fight. I was determined not to run away from the home that Lord Jesus Christ has shown as the place of blessing. My home. My sanctuary.

THE HOLY SPIRIT TAKES OVER

I texted the 'visitors' and said, "*Thank you to Lord Jesus Christ, who has given a mind without fear! I will connect with you.*" Having closed that door, I began to pray. Firstly, it was shaky. Words did not flow like they used to. Then the Holy Spirit spoke in tongues!

My time with the Holy Spirit had its bursts of creativity in art, words, and songs.

The testimony '*JOURNEY OF FAITH: RESPONDING TO GOD'S CALLING*', was an art exhibition with a narrative story. My first book *BRAND NEW YOU IN CHRIST* was published in art and words.

As time passed, the night went from midnight to early morning, and faith began to rise! As I began to declare scriptures and write the words on the walls, a new level of strength came over me. Night-time prayer moved past midnight to a new day.

2 Timothy 1: 7 was the breakthrough scripture. I began to declare the word boldly;

> "*God has not given Chandrika Maelge a spirit of fear! God has given Chandrika Maelge a spirit of power, love, and a sound mind!*"

The more I heard the words, the more I believed in what the words said. I trusted God, I trusted His word. The powerful scripture was a bright light in the darkness. I began to remember who I am in Christ Jesus. I began to remember who my God is. How God has always helped me and stretched His hand in time of need. As per Romans 8:39, I was assured that nothing could separate me from the love of God which is in the Lord Jesus Christ. With this truth, faith moved up like a thermometer put in hot water.

Early morning, I contacted the church that knew me the best. I knew in my heart the pastor; his wife and the church intercessory prayer team would pray for me.

I SENT A PRAYER REQUEST.

I need agreement of prayer for my life's protection.

- Pray for the protection of my home and land.
- Pray for the protection of my mother, aunt, and all pets.
- Rebuke and cancel dark forces trying to gain access through fear.

I am asking this as I am alone, but I know I have true brothers and sisters in Christ Jesus to stand with me. Due to absolute ignorance, I let people enter my home and speak against the atmosphere of the house. Terrible words were spoken.

Any other single woman would have gotten terrified and run away abandoning the house. I was terrified, but I did bounce back as God is good. Since last night I have been requesting co-operation in prayer.

Having sent the text, I told my mother,

"I am fasting today, don't disturb me".

Thereafter, I took my notebooks. I re-read the study notes of the online teachings I had listened to, in November 2023. In early November, as I was strolling through online teachings, my attention was drawn to the teachings and prayer services by an apostle. The apostle lifted his people with his powerful teachings. The messages delivered were powerful and timely. He explained in great detail. It felt customized to me. He taught a lot about prayer, grace, favor, destiny, honor, open doors, and the prophetic. I listened and absorbed the spoken word like a sponge! I practiced what was preached.

My prayer life was elevated.

At the end of his sermons, he prayed over the gathering, releasing uplifting prophetic words. Powerful prophetic declarations were made.

At times, I could feel a vibration entering my hands.

One day, while I was listening to his teachings on restoration and how God lifts men, I burst into a new song of prophetic declaration.

RESTORED BY THE LORD I AM LIFTED UP
WOMEN OF THE WORD I AM LIFTED UP
RESTORED BY THE LORD I AM LIFTED UP
BLESSINGS IN DUE SEASON MY TIME IS NOW
RESTORED BY THE LORD I AM LIFTED UP
TO PREACH THE GOOD NEWS MY TIME IS NOW
RESTORED BY THE LORD I AM LIFTED UP

I believe, the Holy Spirit led me to listen and learn from this apostle, to prepare me for things to come. Later that month, as I faced the spirit of fear head-on, I began to sing the song of restoration. I sang, "*Restored by the Lord I am lifted up!*"

As I sang out prophetically, a great confidence came over me. With that start the Holy Spirit burst into songs. I could feel great energy and strength, just by singing in tongues. Thus, I began fighting for my destiny, as the worship songs played in the background. I began to voice out every prophetic promise released over me. I began to declare the word of God with great power. Words just began to burst out in declarations, with absolute trust in God. Deep inside of me, I knew God was helping me!

With this, the Holy Spirit led me on a prayer and worship marathon.

PRAYER AND WORSHIP MARATHON

That day the Holy Spirit led me, first to rectify my mistakes. I had opened doors that needed to be shut. So, I moved to the gates and repented in prayer.

I REPENT MY LORD! I REPENT!
THIS IS YOUR LAND YOUR HOME
I WELCOME YOU LORD
I WELCOME YOU TO STAY!

Then, I firmly shut the gates, saying "*Doors that Lord Jesus Christ shut no one can* open" (Revelations 3:7). I moved inside the house, repeated the same action, and shut the doors.

I came to the TV lounge area where all evil was spoken. My flesh was still feeling uneasy, yet I began to pray courageously.

1. I prayed in tongues.
2. I prayed, thanking and praising God.
3. I wrote scriptures on walls and prayed.
4. I made bold prophetic declarations.
5. I sang songs gifted by the Holy Spirit.
6. I prayed with the Holy Bible scriptures.
7. I picked up my shawls of purple, red, and blue, and danced with joy with a fresh wind!

#

Psalm 20:5
New Living Translation
[5] May we shout for joy when we hear
of your victory and raise a victory
banner in the name of our God. May
the Lord answer all your prayers.

**AT THAT MOMENT I DID NOT HAVE A BANNER
WITH ME, BUT I HAD MY SHAWLS!** I LIFTED
MY SHAWLS OF PURPLE, RED, AND BLUE AND
BEGAN TO DANCE AND SING, SWIRLING THE
SHAWLS. **VICTORY BANNERS OF PURPLE,
RED AND BLUE!** LORD HAD GIVEN ME NEW
STRENGTH, CONFIDENCE AND BOLDNESS.
I WAS BURSTING WITH JOY. THAT DAY
THE HOLY SPIRIT BIRTHED A NEW WAY OF
WORSHIP FOR ME. **WORSHIP THAT LOOKED
LIKE A VISUAL ARTS DANCE PERFORMANCE.
MIX OF PRAYER, SONG AND DANCE.**

#

My friends say I am a creative person. I did drama, art, dancing, singing, and oratory at school. Being creative in the corporate sector gave me an advantage in my chosen field of marketing, branding, and communications.

The Holy Spirit will remind us of what Lord Jesus Christ spoke, and help us (John 14: 26). There is a relationship aspect to the Holy Spirit. In my walk with Lord Jesus Christ, often I am reminded of God's goodness and moved to prayer and worship of thanksgiving, for the wonderful things God has done in my life. This time, the Holy Spirit reminded me that as a child I used to sing, dance and worship; praising the Lord.

This was how the Heavenly Father had seen me worship as a child!

I followed Buddhism as my religion at school, yet I loved Christian worship. I sang both *Bakthi Geetha* (Buddhist songs) and Christian worship songs. Often, during the interval or a free period, I would go alone to the school chapel and dance and sing. Having witnessed me dance and sing at the school chapel on numerous days, a Christian teacher asked me if I would like to follow Christianity.

I ran away saying, "*I am a Buddhist.*"

I was only nine years of age.

God began to speak in dreams and visions,
during a great sad period, in my life.

The first dream I had in my early thirties, had a curly haired young girl in a white dress and a blue ribbon skipping around the fire. She said,

"Sing for my Father, my Father
wants you to sing for Him."

Praying in tongues, writing, drawing, dancing, and singing Holy Spirit songs, are part of the worship lifestyle, the Holy Spirit had developed in me over the years. It was this worship lifestyle that was elevated on the prayer and worship marathon day.

As I worshipped, led by the Holy Spirit, I felt supercharged. There was immense joy, expressed in a celebratory dance. With this new visual arts kind of worship, I moved from room to room, releasing blessings and declaring words. With the help of the Holy Spirit, I began to win back the territory.

The more I worshiped as led by the Holy Spirit, speaking in tongues and declaring God's promises, the more I was set free from the shackles of fear that imprisoned my mind.

The defeated mind of fear was
replaced by great courage and joy.

I boldly shut the doors and took the keys to my bedroom and the cluttered room. I took my charcoal pencil and began to write on top of the exterior doors and windows. I wrote, having faith in the word in Revelation 3:7, *"Doors that Lord Jesus Christ shut no one can open! No one can enter."* When I did this, a great sense of peace, calm, and assurance came over me, that Jesus Christ the Lord is in control.

The joy and peace at that moment is indescribable.

Have you ever been trapped in an elevator? I have. It's no fun. Even though it was minutes and seconds, it felt like ages. Million thoughts rushed in at the same time. It's worse when the electricity goes off. The mind gets cluttered with the traffic of thoughts, blinking red and amber. But when the lights flickered back on, and you hear the familiar sound of the elevator starting up, immediately there is great relief.

The previous day I felt like being trapped in an elevator with no electricity.

Not only was I trapped in a closed dark cage without visibility. This one seems to be falling. The air inside was suffocating. My heart rate increased. I was running out of air to breathe. Breathless and gasping for air, I could not speak!

It was the worst panic attack I had ever had.

However, when *'little faith'* went into action and got the church praying for me, faith began to build up. As my faith moved up, I began praying and worshipping my God. All other factors just aligned with one accord with one objective, crush the spirit of fear and sing songs of praise and victory. *"Go on C, win back the territory!"*

The manner in which I was delivered from the spirit of fear was very personal to me. The Holy Spirit gets very personal.

I WROTE ON WALLS

My mother told me that, like most children, I drew on walls. In my life, writing and drawing on walls became one of my art forms. In 2015, I was led to write and draw the *'JOURNEY OF FAITH'* on my bedroom walls. Dreams, visions, prophecies, and corresponding Holy Bible scriptures, were creatively put together in my bedroom wall using charcoal. When the Holy Spirit led me to do the testimony in art and words in 40 days in 2017, I only had to look at my bedroom wall! A ten-year journey in faith was up on the wall.

David wrote Psalm 142 in the cave.

Psalm 142 is a prayer. Here, David is crying out to the LORD, lifting his voice to the LORD (Psalm 142:1). He poured his heart out about his troubles (Psalm 142:2).

I can relate. In my darkest and deepest despair, I turned to God for help. I believe in my heart, that God heard my prayers and helped me! I was drowning and choking in fear. I was all alone and felt like being pushed into a deep pit. As I cried out, trusting God, I truly believe, that God heard my cry and the cries of my prayer partners and miraculously helped to set me free from the spirit of fear. I had never seen that might, that courage, that boldness before. It was not my doing! I wrote the scripture of victory 2 Timothy 1:7 in my new writer's space.

Like a child, I wrote on the walls.

I DANCED AND WORSHIPED

Psalmist writes, "You have turned my mourning into joyful dancing" (Psalm 30:11 NLT). As per Exodus 15:20-21, Prophetess Miriam together with the other women began to dance with musical instruments. She sang a song of praise to the LORD for the victory. I am a woman well into my 40s. On the prayer and worship marathon day, I began to sing and dance with the wind in my hair, joyfully swirling the shawls like flags with a fresh wind. That day, I felt like the little girl of 9 years dancing and singing at the school chapel.

I remembered that young curly haired angel singing and dancing for the Father!

A childlike dance for the Father!

A woman dancing with joy, a dance of celebration. Celebrating the deliverance from the spirit of fear.

I SPOKE IN A LOUD VOICE

I did drama during my school days. We did not use microphones in those days. One had to speak in a loud and clear voice. On that day declarations were made firmly and strongly. Not a shout, but with a tone of absolute confidence in the WORD OF GOD that was spoken. The tone of voice in blessing people was more intimate, soft, and loving. I believe the tone of my voice changed based on the words spoken. Tonality in delivering the word has changed. The voice changed!

Fear was no more. In place of timidity; boldness was born.

On my day of deliverance; firstly, the church prayed and continued to make prayers on my behalf to God. Secondly, I prayed, made declarations, and worshipped. I trusted God to help me. What may look questionable, foolish, or even childish to some was the act of worship that looked like a visual art dance performance. This worship just happened.

As the Holy Spirit moved me, my hands moved like a bird flying. The shawls too moved in harmony dancing to the wind. I felt light like a feather harmoniously moving with the wind. It felt as if all those chains that were weighing me down had vanished. Replacing prison shackles was absolute freedom, joy, and peace.

To see a grown woman singing, dancing, speaking in an unknown language, and swirling the shawls, might look questionable and weird in the eyes of the world. I am grateful for the big garden and big gates. I was well hidden from the world's eye. The only witnesses on that day were the animals and giant trees. His creation stood witness, as I broke free from the prison of fear! I was set free from the spirit of fear to live free in the life I am called to live in Christ Jesus. I have been delivered from the spirit of fear!

God, I am grateful!

5 hours of non-stop prayer and worship and I took back the keys to my mind.

Having finished journaling the events of the day, late evening, I broke fast.

I believe it was faith in action by many intercessory prayer warriors and the Holy Spirit led prayer and worship by the believer, which was offered to God trusting Him to help; that resulted in the deliverance from the spirit of fear.

The following day was a Sunday. I visited a gathering that prayed for me.

As I immersed myself in cooperate worship, heavenly visions flooded in. It was wonderful to worship with my fellow brothers and sisters in Christ. All my inhibitions have vanished. I worshipped rejoicing and thanking God! I danced, whilst worshipping with absolute joy. During worship, God gave me a new vision for the new season. The mist had cleared and I could see.

In the days to follow; I began cleaning the unclean room full of junk. The atmosphere was cleansed with worship songs, prophetic declarations, and praying in the spirit. It was in that messy room the Holy Spirit nudged me to start writing the testimony. Nearly three months later the room is brand new with fresh paint and refreshed interiors. A painting of a lighthouse adorns the room.

It is noteworthy to mention that the after-effects of the spirit of fear's attack, did last for a few weeks. Strange things happened. In addition, someone carried a message, saying that someone else had seen my home flooded with blood. However, this time around, words of wisdom cancelled the words intended to cause fear. Having ended the conversation, I went and prayed boldly with the WORD OF GOD. I firmly stood my ground that fear is not from God.

I fear not! THANK YOU, GOD!

OVERCOMER'S CHECKLIST

A trial, a text triumphed with, Lord Jesus Christ results in life lessons that can help others. The Holy Spirit led me to journal, learnings from the testimony FEAR TO GLORY. Let me share it with you.

LESSON LEARNT:

Stop reacting to words! Don't take everything into the heart.

Proverbs 4:23, instructs Christians to painstakingly guard their hearts, as all life's issues will arise from the heart.

Pay attention to the spoken words. Guard your heart from negative words. Receive the words that build faith. Reject the words that torment, oppress and cause fear. Cross-check and examine any prophetic word with others and the word of God. Politely, put a stop to negative, stressful or abusive conversations. If that's not possible, remove yourselves from that environment. Earnestly, pray for yourself to let no bitterness and offense take root in your heart. Also, be responsible for the words spoken by you.

Daily ask the Holy Spirit to give you words in dealing with people.

LESSON LEARNT:

Arise from words and situations, which weigh you down and activate prayer.

As per Isaiah 60:1, a Christian, should rise and shine.

First, recognize what you need to arise from. It can be depression, fear, anxiety, worry, poverty, stagnation or any other situation that is weighing you down. The start of overcoming is to recognize the issue. Thereafter, one needs to apply the word of God to that situation. If you are unable to receive words via prayers and revelations, then research, with keywords. If you are too afraid to do any of this; reach out to a prayer partner.

Pray! Pray! Pray!

LESSON LEARNT:

When your flesh is irritated, stop! Run to God!

Remember Exodus 14:14, "The Lord will fight for you, and you shall hold[a] your peace" (NKJV).

Avoid taking any action, when you are physically and/or emotionally challenged. Often decisions made in haste driven by emotion are mostly driven by flesh. Once fleshly emotions take the upper hand in a challenging situation, those emotions will trigger negative actions. These actions may lead you to sin.

Actions triggered by negative thoughts naturally lead to something unpleasant. Stop panicking. Calm down. Play some worship songs to create a good positive atmosphere. One needs a calm and sound mind to see clearly and act out with wisdom. Spend some time with the Holy Spirit, before you leap from one emotion to another. So be still, surrender it all to God.

Present your case to your Father God.

LESSON LEARNT:

Prayerfully, choose your spiritual mentors.

In 1 Corinthians 11:1, Apostle Paul makes a statement to follow him as an example, just as he follows Christ.

Most often, we tend to love our Christian leaders with unfailing love. Unconsciously, one tends to glorify the man and defend his actions. Has one begun to follow man blindly? If we are blinded by our own emotions, we may let anyone speak and mentor us.

Keep watch for signs or words of intimidation, fear, control and domination.

We are to follow those who follow Christ (1 Corinthians 11:1). We must look for the character of Lord Jesus Christ in those who we choose to follow. Be mindful that no one is perfect!

It is good to love and honour our Christian leaders. However, not everyone can be your spiritual mentor. Ask the Holy Spirit to lead you to your spiritual mentor; who will help you in your journey in faith.

Prayerfully and mindfully, build on a fruitful mentorship with Lord Jesus Christ being the head of both mentor and protegee, and the word of God being the light of guidance.

LESSON LEARNT:

Be very selective of the voices you choose to speak to you.

The LORD warns us through prophet Jeremiah, to stop listening to certain prophets who make up things and speak, giving false hope. For they do not speak for the LORD (Jeremiah 23:16).

Cross-examine the word of advice to the Word of God.

Ask yourself the question, does it agree with what God is saying? Will the action cause me to sin or glorify God? Do your research. Don't accept everything spoken as prophecy. Do what glorifies God! Bin all that leads to sin!

LESSON LEARNT:

Be conscious of the thoughts you entertain.

There is a need to change the way we think (Ephesians 4:23). When your mind starts to run its race of thoughts; take control to put the stop sign in the traffic of thoughts. Every day ask the Holy Spirit to take control of your thoughts, feelings and imaginations, and align all with God's purposes and will. In Matthew 15:13, Jesus says *"Every plant which My heavenly Father has not planted will be uprooted"* (NKJV). Therefore, ask God to uproot fear, anxiety, worry and doubts at the start itself. Do not allow these plants to become trees.

A mind controlled by the Holy Spirit will think about what pleases the Spirit (Romans 8:5).

Ask the Holy Spirit to lead you and take control of all thoughts, actions and emotions.

LESSON LEARNT:

Love and pray for those who hurt you.

Lord Jesus Christ teaches us to love our enemies, and to pray for them (Matthew 5:44). I had an issue of the heart of unforgiveness and a writer's block period of nearly two months. I could not write a word! It was a period of forgiving and healing. The Holy Spirit led me on an intense and painful time of moving my heart from hurt to love. Forgiving those who hurt you is for your peace.

Colossians 3:13 instructs Christians, to forgive each other, as the Lord forgave us.

Healing can only begin with forgiveness, love, and prayer for those who have wronged you.

The victory of being set free from the spirit of fear brought me to a new journey of healing. Healing is a process.

Face to face with betrayal and hurt by people who I trusted and loved, I ran to the Father God, who healed my brokenness. It was buckets of tears one after the other. With prayer and many tears for those who hurt me, I asked God to intervene in their lives. I kept praying. For some, it was to be led to salvation. To another, it was to soften the heart by the Holy Spirit, for the Lord to have His way. To another, it was to come to peace with their calling.

As I truly began praying for those who hurt me, new words started to flood the prayer life. As a result, I was led to edit afresh the words of this book. With a fresh set of eyes and prayer notes in hand, I edited the context of the book over the next two months.

LESSON LEARNT:

Submit all things to God each day.

James 4:7, advises the Christian to submit to the Lord.

There is a constant battle between the flesh and the Spirit within us, on a daily basis. Make it your daily prayer point to ask the Holy Spirit to guide you, lead you and, enable you to action the will of God. All will not go smoothly; your flesh will constantly be at a tug-a-war with the Spirit. However, when you consciously submit, it starts to get better. Submit all things to the Lord and believe He the Lord is in control of your day.

When you surrender it all to the Lord,
be prepared for drastic changes.

LESSON LEARNT:

Be bold! Be courageous! Start living out, your God given purpose.

According to Romans 8:28 (NLT), "And we know that God causes everything to work together[a] for the good of those who love God and are called according to his purpose for them."

Develop a hunger within you to see, God's plans and purposes for you become a reality here on earth.

Begin to recognize how God brings all things, this includes people, resources and the environment for good, so that you live out His purpose here on earth! Amen.

WORDS OF ENCOURAGEMENT

This chapter elaborates on INTERCESSORY PRAYER, WORSHIP LED BY THE HOLY SPIRIT, and FIGHT WITH WORDS; which were at the core of this testimony of deliverance from the spirit of fear.

I hope that these words will benefit you, as you journey in faith.

In 2015, a pastor in Sri Lanka told me; *"IT'S A PROGRESSIVE PERIOD OF ART OF MINISTRY, YOU WILL WRITE BOOKS."* In 2017, a pastor from the USA called me out as the *"WOMAN OF THE WORD"*. Then another prophesied, *"MY LIFE WILL BE A BOOK"*. In 2017, the Holy Spirit nudged me to present the journey of faith in responding to God's calling in art and words, an art exhibition with a written narrative. This was the humble beginning of sharing practical Christianity.

In October 2016, I was encouraged by Psalm 96: 3, "Publish his glorious deeds among the nations. Tell everyone about the amazing things he does "(NLT). Therefore, I continue to write.

BE ENCOURAGED!

INTERCESSORY PRAYER

When your FAITH is facing the onslaught of a great massive tsunami, what would you do?

You pray. If you just can't pray, please call the intercessory prayer hotline!

All churches have a group of people who carry a special grace for prayer. They are burdened to pray for others. Most churches have an intercessory prayer group. Ensure, you cultivate good friendships with a few powerful intercessory prayer warriors, who command an audience in the throne room of God. When you are down and low, they will be the ones pounding on heaven's doors on your behalf.

The Christian needs an entourage that encourages and builds faith as the Christian navigates through the journey in faith. According to 1 Timothy 2:1, a Christian should prioritize prayer and praying for others. Praying for others is every Christian's responsibility. When I could not pray, it was the prayers of the intercessors that built faith in me. Prayers can encourage and build faith.

I am led to participate in intercessory prayer groups. I am driven, especially to pray for the church together with other intercessors, who share my burden.

I began writing this book because firstly the Holy Spirit nudged me to start writing, and thereafter, I was encouraged by an intercessory prayer warrior. She is super busy with her own work and ministry work. Yet, she found time to send messages, voice cuts of prayers, make a quick call, and often have a chat on the progress of the book. She would explain the pruning process and the need to keep editing. We somehow found time to connect.

If I am to testify to the power of prayer, I will have to write a separate book (big grin).

In short, I have seen widows and single mothers helped in ways one cannot rationalize, simply because they prayed. I have seen deadly diseases leave the host, simply because the church prayed. I have seen people's lives extended when a prayer intercessor prayed. I have seen court cases resolved as the church prayed. I have seen the word of faith in prayer give a fresh new lease of life to a dead-dying situation. I have seen on-the-spot miracle healings simply because the believer activated faith and prayed. I have seen victory in many trials, simply because someone was praying with me or praying for me.

You may be a mighty prayer warrior, but trust me there are times you may need the prayers of others.

A PRISONER WAS SET FREE

*The spirit of fear can only terrorize
you if you give it access.*

In my case, the mistakes I made, and the doors I opened, allowed the spirit of fear to attack me. If one is under the spirit of fear, one must be set free from the prison of fear and be delivered. You must break free from the self-imposed prison of the mind and win back the keys to your mind!

Break free from the prison of fear!

In the New Testament, we come across instances where Lord Jesus Christ's apostles were set free from physical prisons in mysterious manners. In one instance, the church was praying, and a miracle took place in the prison (reference, Acts 12: 5-10). Let us look at the story of Peter the Apostle being set free from prison.

WHAT WAS THE SCENARIO?

King Harold was persecuting the church (Acts 12: 1). Peter was arrested by King Harold and was put in prison, guarded by four squadrons of soldiers (Acts 12: 4).

Peter was in prison and was well-guarded!

I was held captive in my mind by the spirit of fear. My mind was locked up and fear had taken the keys. The fearful mind immobilized me. I could not pray. In addition, I was persecuted by tormenting spirits. I was a prisoner of my mind.

WHO PRAYED?

Peter was in prison and the church earnestly interceded and offered prayers to God, for Peter (Acts: 12:5). I believe, God sent help from heaven to Peter because the church kept earnestly praying to God on behalf of Peter.

I was terrified at the start, that I could not pray. However, 'little faith' in me, reached out to others who in turn, prayed to God on my behalf. The church prayed and interceded for me. Prayers of others gave me the start to pray!

WHAT WAS THE DIVINE INTERVENTION?

As per Acts 12:7, a light was seen in the prison, and the angel of the Lord was seen standing near Peter. This angel woke Peter and raised him and the chains on Peter's hands fell off him.

According to Acts 12:10, the angel and Peter went past the two guard posts and came to the gates that led to the city. The gates to the city opened by itself. Once they came onto the street, the angel immediately left Peter.

It was a prison break by divine intervention.

I did not see angels on the day of deliverance. However, I was given great strength, boldness, and courage, which I never knew before. I believe in my situation, God intervened and brought about the deliverance from the spirit of fear, and with it a great new level of boldness and courage.

WHAT WAS THE END RESULT?

Once Peter was set free from prison. Peter visited the house of prayer (Acts 12:12). Peter told them what the Lord had done to set him free from prison, and he requested that they go tell James and others of the things that had happened (Acts 12: 17).

Peter shared his testimony.

As for myself, I was set free from fear's prison. I was delivered from the spirit of fear. Also, the mind's gates to the tormenting spirits were shut. Led by the Holy Spirit, I too visited a church that prayed to God on my behalf and thereafter, began writing this book to testify and give glory to God. In my testimony, two sets of prayers reached God on that day. The personal heart cry of the believer (my prayers) Intercessory prayers by the church (these are the many prayer teams). I thank God, for the many intercessory prayer warriors who prayed on my behalf.

Just the thought of knowing; that my brothers and sisters in Christ were making prayers on my behalf, gave me hope and great strength.

As the day progressed, I kept in touch with a few prayer intercessors via a quick text. We agreed and cooperated in prayer.

So much faith was activated!

We know that, without faith, one cannot please God (Hebrews 11:6).

Initially, the believer's faith (i.e.: my faith) was very low. However, with the prayers of the intercessors, faith was built up. As the intercessors kept praying, my faith moved to new levels.

These divine interventions are often questioned by many. According to 1 Corinthians 2:14, spiritual things are often considered foolish by those who are without the Holy Spirit. I believe in miracles. I have witnessed many encounters.

I believe God intervened on that day to set me free from the spirit of fear; because prayers were made in faith trusting God to help! Also, it is God's nature to help His children, when they call Him!

A FEW GOOD HABITS TO DEVELOP

Do you have a prayer partner? Are you a member of a prayer group? Is there an intercessor praying for you? Then you are truly blessed.

Here are a few good habits to cultivate:

- Get involved in the prayer ministry of your local church.
- Participate in both physical and online meetings on prophetic/intercessory prayer.
- Develop good friendships with your intercessory prayer partners.
- Reach out to prayer groups, especially when you are unable to pray.
- Pray for your intercessory prayer warriors. Thank God for them and let them pray for you and with you to God.
- Fellowship with your intercessory prayer partners.
- In your own prayer time, pray for others.
- Keep a prayer request journal and thank God for answered prayers, as you tick them one by one.

Asking for prayers is not a weakness.

WORSHIP LED BY THE HOLY SPIRIT!

"God is Spirit, and those who worship Him must worship in spirit and truth" (John 4:24 NKJV). If one is controlled by the Holy Spirit one's thoughts will be that which pleases the Spirit (Romans 8:5). Therefore, the believer's main aim should be to let the Holy Spirit change the way they think (Ephesians 4:23).

Thoughts lead to actions. Actions can become habitual.

According to Romans 8:14, "For as many as are led by the Spirit of God, these are sons of God" (NKJV). Our very identity is established based on the fact, whether or not; we are led by the Holy Spirit.

In the run-up to the prayer and worship marathon day, the Holy Spirit led me on an intense period of refinement and cleansing.

Spontaneous worship of the Holy Spirit birthed songs was very much part of the journey. It was challenging to shed the old and put on the new. My flesh kept falling back to the old. Through repentance, prayer, fasting, worship, and meditation of the word of God, the old skin was shed and new skin began to appear, in all areas of my life.

As per 2 Corinthians 5:17 "*Therefore, if anyone is in Christ, he is a new creation; old things have passed away; behold, all things have become new*" (NKJV). Just like a caterpillar becomes a butterfly, a Christian's life will become something new.

There is a new life in Christ Jesus.

I am not perfect; I am being perfected by the Holy Spirit. I am not the same person I was ten years ago, and I believe I will not be the same person as I am today, in ten years.

At the end of most church services, one hears the words of 2 Corinthians 13:14, "The grace of the Lord Jesus Christ, and the love of God, and the communion of the Holy Spirit be with you all. Amen" (NKJV). There is a very real relationship aspect to the Holy Spirit. The time allocated by the believer for fellowship with the Holy Spirit will result in the richness of the relationship the believer will have with the Holy Spirit. It is very difficult to comprehend the personal relationship aspect of the Holy Spirit for those who do not know the person the Lord Holy Spirit. As per 1 Corinthians 2:14, without the Spirit one cannot understand spiritual things.

The deliverance from the spirit of fear to me is like being set free from prison. Therefore, I have chosen Holy Bible stories of prison breaks by divine intervention to further explain.

PRISONERS WERE SET FREE

Let us look at the Holy Bible story where Paul and Silas were set free from a physical prison. This prison break had worship and divine intervention at its core.

WHAT HAPPENED?

"Around midnight Paul and Silas were praying and singing hymns to God, and the other prisoners were listening" (Acts 16:25 NLT). As per Acts 16:26, a great earthquake happened and shook the prison's foundation, opening all prison doors, and also chains on all prisoners fell off them.

Prayer and worship were made to God, and a miraculous divine intervention took place in prison, setting the prisoners free.

When fear gripped me, I was fortunate to have a brother and sister in Christ who interceded and prayed for me. It resulted in building my faith. I began praying.

With prayer and worship, the time went past midnight into a new day.

As the worship songs played in the background, the Holy Spirit moved me into deeper levels of prayer and worship. Then suddenly, I broke into a dance of celebration.

Prayer and worship changed the atmosphere of my home to break open fear's prison gates!

WHAT WAS THE DIVINE INTERVENTION?

According to Acts 16:26; there was a great earthquake, and all prison doors were opened. Also, the prisoner's chains were loosened.

On my day of deliverance, the earth did not shake, but the fear's stronghold was shaken and broken. I was set free from shackles of fear!

WHAT WAS THE END RESULT?

Paul and Silas once set free from prison, immediately engaged in ministry. According to Acts 16: 30 -32; the prison keeper took Paul and Silas outside and asked what he needed to do to be saved. Paul and Silas shared the Lord's word with the prison keeper's household on that day.

The Holy Spirit led me to journal on the prayer and worship marathon, day of fast. The Holy Spirit made me stop and take note of what was done and what happened. When I was led to write the testimony, I already had my reference notes in hand. Once I was set free from the prison of fear, I was led to write, thereby ending years of stagnation since 2020. I thank God for reigniting the fire!

Listen to the Holy Spirit! He will bring to remembrance all that Lord Jesus Christ spoke, and help you (John 14: 26). He will reveal deeper things of God (1 Corinthians 2:10). He will teach the truth (1 John 2:27). Yes! The Holy Spirit will speak through you (Matthew 10:20).

John 4:23

New Living Translation

23 But the time is coming—indeed it's here now—when true worshipers will worship the Father in spirit and in truth. The Father is looking for those who will worship him that way.

My journey of worshiping the Father in spirit and truth began in 2015, with the very first song of cleansing by the Holy Spirit. It was a heart cry to cleanse me in all of my ways, all of my thoughts, all of my words, all of my actions, and my heart, to make me more like my Lord Jesus Christ. I would sing, "*You are the God, the Lord Oh mighty, cleanse me Lord, Oh God Oh mighty, make me more like you ....*"

In simple words, character refinement!

It has been nearly ten years. Slowly but surely over these years much has changed. Thank you, Holy Spirit, for leading me to repent and action the change, whenever I fell short.

A Christian must pursue a worship lifestyle birthed by the Holy Spirit, one that refines the character to be brand new in Christ Jesus!

A FEW GOOD HABITS TO DEVELOP

Prayer and worship are at the center of the Book of Psalms. Psalmist says, as long as he lives, he will praise the LORD and sing praises to God (Psalm 146:2). Develop that kind of a worship lifestyle.

Here are a few good habits to cultivate:

- Daily play worship songs/shofar sounds/ prophetic worship etc.
- Find the Psalm that best relates to your situation and recite it with your name in it.
- Close your eyes, let go of your control, and let the Holy Spirit lead you in worship. Sing!
- Start speaking in tongues; better yet start singing in tongues.
- Ask the Holy Spirit to cleanse you in all of your ways, words, and thoughts. Make it your heart cry. Pursue holiness!
- Let worship songs play as background music as you work, as you drive etc. Be conscious!
- Always thank and praise God in psalms and hymns. Rejoice!

Dance as you worship! Let the Holy Spirit lead you!

FIGHT WITH WORDS

The spirit of fear entered my mind, BY WAY OF WORDS and imprisoned my mind.

I opened many doors for many voices to speak into my life and entertained all kinds of stories, which contributed to opening a door for fear. I pinch myself today, and say out loud, *"The Holy Spirit had warned you. You forgot! Why did you open the door?"*

Fear kept me in chains. I felt unproductive and empty.

Once fear entered the mind, it made way for many other negative spirits to enter the mind, creating great chaos as explained in the PERSONAL TESTIMONY. Also elaborated in the testimony, is the *'little faith'* that went into action with humility asking for prayers from brothers and sisters in Christ. With intercessory prayer, my faith began to rise! Thereafter, the Holy Spirit took over and led me on a prayer and worship marathon, engaging in spiritual warfare against the enemy's powers, schemes, and plans.

I did not run in fright! Instead, I stood my ground, and was led to fight with words, activating faith!

The Christian should fight a good fight of faith (1 Timothy 6:12). After all, the Christian is on a JOURNEY OF FAITH.

How does one fight with faith?

One must believe and trust in the WORD OF GOD, and put that trust into action. For our trust should be in the power of God (1 Corinthians 2:5). Let me remind you, it was words that caused fear in me, and it was words that won the battle. Highlighted below, are three areas the Holy Spirit moved me to fight with faith in words.

1. SPEAKING IN TONGUES
2. DECLARATIONS
3. FIGHT WITH PROPHETIC WORDS

1. SPEAKING IN TONGUES

At the start, fear gripped me so tight, I could not breathe. At that moment, I could not put a sentence together in prayer. I was terrified! When faith began to arise, the Holy Spirit took charge, and I began speaking in tongues.

Over the last decade, the Holy Spirit led me to speak in tongues in private, especially, when I faced a challenging situation. At times, it was a brisk prayer walk praying in tongues or a silent utterance in a closed-up cubicle. It came as no surprise to me that the prayer marathon kickstarted with prayer warfare, praying in tongues.

I am glad the Holy Spirit took over with utterance.

According to Romans 8:26, the Holy Spirit intercedes for us with groaning; when we don't know what to pray. Tongues spoken on that day were like going to war. In tongues, I engaged in warfare prayers in the Spirit. As per 1 Corinthians 14:4, speaking in tongues encourages the individual who speaks it. True to the scripture, I was built up as I spoke in tongues.

Whenever you feel weak, build yourselves by speaking in tongues! According to, 1 Corinthians 14:2, when we speak in tongues we are speaking to God, man cannot understand the utterance; for it is mysteries we speak in spirit. For a moment, pause and think, how wonderful, God's ways are. He has given us a powerful gift to build ourselves. Speaking in tongues is a gift of the Holy Spirit (1 Corinthians 12:10). Put the gift of speaking in tongues into good use, daily and build capacity.

2. DECLARATIONS

In the Old Testament, often God tells His people to be strong and courageous (Joshua 1:6; cf. Deuteronomy 31:6). In fact, Joshua is commanded by the LORD, "This is my command— be strong and courageous! Do not be afraid or discouraged. For the Lord your God is with you wherever you go." (Joshua 1:9 NLT).

Fear and discouragement seem to be the main negative factors that can attack the Christian's journey in faith. Fear can choke out courage and hope. Many are slaves to fear! The word of God that broke open the prison gates of fear is 2 Timothy 1:7. To counter the spirit of fear; God has given us the spirit of power, love, and sound mind (2 Timothy 1:7)

2 Timothy 1:7
New King James Version
[7] For God has not given us a spirit of fear, but of power and of love and a sound mind.

LOVE

The first truth the Holy Spirit brought to my remembrance is that I cannot be separated from the love of God found in Christ Jesus (John 14: 26, Romans 8:39). It was a flashback moment of all the goodness of God throughout the last decade in my life. How good and loving my Father God has been to me. How Lord Jesus Christ's grace, has helped me to overcome many challenges. I recalled how the word of God in declaration in faith has brought many victories in my life.

This truth alone put a full stop to the panic and calmed the mind.

Fear cannot rise up against the love of God. According to 1 John 4: 18, perfect love has the ability to chase out fear.

God loves you! Remember that always!

SOUND MIND

Having a sound mind is critical to face and triumph over any challenge. The spirit of fear attacks the mind and keeps it in prison. Fear creates great chaos in the mind. It's a battle within.

Isaiah 41:10 is a good encouragement scripture to refresh your mind in challenging situations. According to Isaiah 41:10, God is with us, God helps us, and He promises to strengthen us and lift us with His righteous right hand.

As per 1 Corinthians 2:16, the believers have the mind of Christ. Ask yourself,

"So why fear?"

We are still in our mortal bodies. A person's body and mind are subjected to various stresses. Fear entered as one opened a door. Therefore, one needs to consciously watch out, as to what enters the mind and what habits are being formed. A good start would be to allow the Spirit to renew our thoughts and attitudes (Ephesians 4:23).

The best way to protect the mind is to fill the mind with the word of God. Just think! If your mind is full of the truth of the scriptures, would you become afraid? Also, it is best not to dwell on past mistakes and past sins.

Declutter the mind and fill it with the promises of God. It is written in 2 Timothy 1:7, that God has given us a sound mind.

I fear not! Let that mind be in you.

POWER:

Various anxieties, worries, and fears can trap the mind in a prison cell. Fear is the worst of them. When fear enters the mind; it creates room for all other negative spirits to enter as explained in the testimony.

When the Holy Spirit comes upon the believer, the believer will receive power (Acts 1:8). It is the Holy Spirit that enables us with power to speak the word of God with great boldness (Acts 4:31).

Many overcomers pay tribute in their testimonies to the Holy Spirit, who enabled them. Empowerment by the Holy Spirit is easy to understand, when one has an intimate relationship with the Holy Spirit, where the Holy Spirit has enabled great breakthroughs and helped overcome life's many trials. In my journey of faith, the Holy Spirit has always empowered me to do things I thought were impossible and helped me overcome many trials. I truly believe the Holy Spirit empowered me to defeat the spirit of fear. I am conscious of seeking the guidance and direction of the Holy Spirit daily. The Holy Spirit will help accomplish one's assignment here on earth.

The Holy Spirit empowers the believer!

3. FIGHT WITH PROPHETIC WORDS

The ability to prophesy is a gift by the Holy Spirit (1 Corinthians 12:10).

As you journey in faith, you will come across a few who will speak prophecies over your life. If you journal these words of prophecies, you will identify some of them are speaking the same thing in different words.

Apostle Paul encourages young Timothy; "Timothy, my son, here are my instructions for you, based on the prophetic words spoken about you earlier. May they help you fight well in the Lord's battles" (1 Timothy 1:18 NLT).

I believe the prophetic word edifies and lifts the believer (1 Corinthians 14:3).

On the prayer and worship marathon day, faith in the prophetic was put into action through declarations, and voicing out the prophecies spoken over me over the years. It felt as if I was fighting for my life, the very destiny of my life. The recollection of the prophetic words encouraged me. I firmly believe we need to prophesy on ourselves using the Holy Bible scriptures.

Go on and declare what God is saying. Trust God! Act in faith!

A FEW GOOD HABITS TO DEVELOP

For the Christian to fight with words, the Christian needs a good foundation and understanding of the WORD OF GOD. There needs to be a hunger to know God, to know Lord Jesus Christ, and to know the person Lord Holy Spirit.

To dive deeper I enrolled in theological studies, at a Christian seminary. Here are a few good habits to cultivate:

- Daily, study the word of God and make notes.
- Build yourself daily by declaring God's promises.
- Daily spend quality time with the Holy Spirit.
- Daily speak in tongues and worship.
- Maintain a journal, to record encounters, revelations, and any specific instructions by the Holy Spirit.
- By faith run with the prophetic. A prophecy usually will have conditions. Action by faith, what is required.
- Be builders of faith, and encourage others with the Holy Bible scriptures.

Pray! Now fight with the word of God!

JOURNEY CONTINUES

My life has changed drastically, over the last couple of months.

I can confidently say, that the Holy Spirit produced much fruit, in endurance, self-control, love, joy, and peace, which needed sprouting out in me, during this assignment (Galatians 5:22-23). I am positive that with the next assignment, the Holy Spirit will produce even greater fruit.

I am burdened to write this message.

The area I would like to elaborate is on spiritual mentorship.

Firstly, I am a mentor. I am a builder of people and ministries. My manual of mentorship is the Holy Bible. I have benefited greatly from great men and women of God, who have guided me, in my walk with Lord Jesus Christ. I believe we need sound counsel, as we journey in faith. Having said this, one must be very conscious in selecting who speaks over one's life. Do not rush to agree to mentorship opportunities. Do not decide on a mentor, based on familiarity, friendship, and emotion.

WAIT! I say to myself; "I do not rush!"

Pray about it. Earnestly, ask God to connect you with His chosen mentors.

Spiritual mentorship is required as one journey in faith. God knows who is best for you. Let God separate you from relationships that are not from Him. Also, humble yourself, and connect with those God has placed in your life to accomplish the assignment, He has entrusted to you.

Prayerfully identify, the destiny helpers God has placed in your life.

Often when we need help, we usually turn to our network. Over the years I have noticed, God's grace has come in unusual ways for me. God has always connected me to the right people at the right time to accomplish what He has placed in my heart. Some of them were my friends, who graciously invested time and resources to help me. This time, the Holy Spirit taught me to look beyond my surroundings. In the process of writing the book, I was made aware of the destiny helpers that God placed in my life for this assignment. God placed a teacher of Christian theology and a Holy Spirit filled apostle, whose teachings edified, inspired, and lifted me. The topics they taught felt tailormade to me. God placed a Holy Spirit led prayer partner, who shouldered my burdens, encouraged me, and gently guided me.

When the assignment is from God, He brings His entourage of destiny helpers to accomplish the task at hand. We don't have to go looking for them. These are Holy Spirit led divine connections.

> *To be honest, I wondered, why did I have to go through this spiritual attack? Why did God allow it?*

After the deliverance. I thought all was well. But it was not so. Some laughed at me, others mocked me, and others wanted to test the spirit. I simply ignored it and I got busy writing. I am looking ahead, moving on without a rearview mirror for past mistakes. In my quiet time of prayer, the Holy Spirit reveals that the testimonies of an overcomer are for the benefit of others. It is to bring glory to God, a good Father who is always there to lift His children when they call upon Him.

> *Often, prayer intercessors are burdened for the church, God's people, and the country. I share this burden.*

The Holy Spirit filled and empowered body of Christ is the answer to a suffering world. The enemy looks for opportunities to attack the church as an institution and the church as the people of God. We intercede and make petitions to God concerning the church.

In one accord we ask God to protect and strengthen the churches to shine bright as authentic lights, walking in love, and light of Lord Jesus Christ.

In one Spirit, we ask God to root out, all things that are not of Him from the churches.

We also ask God to remove every cancerous dark force attacking the hearts of His people, birthing desires that are contradictory to God's will for them. I wait with hope, as I can see God raising voices who boldly preach and warn the body of Christ, who reach with love to a suffering world. Most of these churches and ministries are small. Yet, they have begun to set out in faith, truth, and love.

As for myself, every day feels like a prayer and worship marathon day.

Prayer and worship have become a lifestyle. The new boldness has become part of my character. Spontaneous worship and prayer walks in the garden have re-started. Every meeting, conversation, and visit is submitted to the Lord. Studying the WORD OF GOD, journaling and drawing have once again found their joy. Whenever I feel drained out, I reach out to the network of mighty intercessors.

I have begun to reach out and connect.

My home has become a place of hospitality, a place of rest and joy.

I share this wonderful, blessed home and land with my family, their friends, my friends, and even the random foreigner. My home and sanctuary have become my place of rest, my place of peace, and my place of joy.

REJOICE!

REJOICE! REJOICE! THE LORD IS IN THIS PLACE. (2X)
MY SAVIOR! MY REDEEMER!
MY HELPER! MY PROVIDER!
MY HEALER! MY PROTECTOR!
THE LORD IS IN THIS PLACE!
REJOICE! REJOICE! THE LORD IS IN THIS PLACE. (2X)

It was a Sunday. I had Holy Communion at home. I shared my testimony and the word. I worshiped the new song, rejoicing and praising God!

And it rained!

The word of God says we are transformed into His image, by the Holy Spirit from glory to glory (2 Corinthians 3:18). Fear, worry, anxiety, and panic are not part of the glorious character of Lord Jesus Christ. In fact, Jesus was sleeping through a fearful storm, and his frightened disciples came and woke him up (Matthew 8:24-25). Can we sleep through the storms of life, trusting God to help?

The last four years, my mind was not in a glorious place. Glory was showing in bits and pieces, but it was not constant. My mindset was chaotic, fearful, worrisome, and panicking. For God to promote us from one level of glory to another, the start must be glory. When I look back, I am grateful for the turn of events. I was well hidden in a safe place and the Lord delivered me from a chaotic and fearful mind to give me a mind of peace. Peace is a fruit of the spirit (Galatians 5:22). It's a good place to be.

A door to the spirit of fear was opened, by worrying, about generational curses, witchcraft, and dark forces. Now that these weeds have been uprooted from my mind and the truth is growing nourished daily by the word of God, fear has no place in my mind. All rooms in my mind are now daily being filled by the truth!

I have no more fear! It is a glorious new season. With a brand-new mindset and a spirit of; love, power, and sound mind, I move forward in the journey of faith.

MY MINDSET HAS MOVED FROM CHAOS TO PEACE AND GLORY IN CHRIST JESUS.

PRAISE GOD!

#

DEAR READER,

HAVE A LOOK AT THE FRONT COVER. THE
ART IS TITLED **SHINE YOUR LIGHT.**

THE CHRISTIAN IS TO SHINE THE LIGHT
RECEIVED FROM GOD TO A HURTING
AND BROKEN WORLD. THE CHRISTIAN'S
USER MANUAL IS THE HOLY BIBLE!

The art is inspired by Isaiah 60: 1-2

Isaiah 60:1-2
New Living Translation
"Arise, Jerusalem! Let your light
shine for all to see. For the glory
of the Lord rises to shine on you.
[2] Darkness as black as night covers all
the nations of the earth, but the glory
of the Lord rises and appears over you.

#

CLOSING PRAYER

Post deliverance from the spirit of fear, the Holy Spirit led me to study Romans 12. Having absorbed its words, I was led to pray.

My God my Father, God of all grace, I come before you in the throne room of God, in the name of Jesus Christ the Lord; Father let your children remember that you have given them a spirit of love, power, and sound mind.
Father God, let no one intimidate, control, and dominate your children with fear tactics. Let no one think that they are superior to the other. Let there be no competition and division amongst us.

Father God, let the love of God be seen in all of us in our service. Let us reach out with brotherly love, sisterly love to those who may be weak in faith. Let us be builders of faith in love. Let us build your kingdom with love. Let the ones with the master plan, teach the builders how to build. Let us come together in one accord, one spirit in the unity in Christ Jesus.

Lord Holy Spirit help the children of God to walk with boldness. Lord, give your children the gift of discernment to know what is from God and what is not. Lord Holy Spirit guide the children of God to become, walking epistles of Christ Jesus in the marketplace. In the name of the Lord Jesus Christ, I ask and pray. Amen.

ACKNOWLEDGMENTS

This book is a product of God's goodness, mercy, grace, and love. I faced many challenges throughout the process of writing this book. The Lord strengthened me, kept me safe, and gave me His grace. I am grateful to God for providing in unusual ways and giving me wisdom to manage finances. Thank you, Father God, for loving me, calling me and choosing me. Thank you, for giving me a spirit of power, love, and a sound mind. I thank and praise God in Jesus Christ the Lord's name, for delivering me from the spirit of fear. FATHER GOD, I AM GRATEFUL!

I believe God brings His destiny helpers
to accomplish the God given assignment.
I thank God in Jesus Christ the Lord's
name for His destiny helpers.

I believe the Holy Spirit guided me in November 2023 to listen and act by faith, to what was taught by **Apostle Joshua Selman.** It was the notes from his teachings that I referred to start, the prayer and worship marathon day. Apostle Joshua's prayers and the manner in which he prayed influenced my prayer life. The powerful prophetic declarations lifted me to boldly pray for many hours. I continue to follow his teachings online and receive and act by faith. As a result, I have begun writing and drawing with joy, once again.

Thank you, Apostle Joshua Selman, for lifting me up with your powerful and timely teachings.

Nilmini Gunewardena (Nimmi) was the first respondent to my cry for help. She prayed with a soft, calm, and powerful voice, which silenced the raging chaos in my mind at the start. We constantly kept in touch throughout the process of writing and publishing this book. She gave me the freedom and time to resolve problem areas with the help of the Holy Spirit and also gently guided me like a big sister in Christ. Nimmi patiently read my long messages, listened to my recordings, and encouraged me. Nimmi partnered with prayer throughout the process of writing this book. Life experiences Nimmi had faced were similar to what I was going through in my personal life. Her testimony helped me to move forward trusting God.

Thank you Nimmi, you truly carried my burden and encouraged me.

Dr. Ted Rubesh, it was a delight to follow your lectures. Your words have inspired me, to reword some of my words in this book. I thank you for sharing your in-depth knowledge with joy. Mid last year, a Christian theological seminary gifted me a voucher. I believe the Holy Spirit kept this voucher gathering dust for two terms, just so that I can utilize it in a term, you happened to be teaching on Old Testament Prophets.

Thank you, Dr. Ted Rubesh, your teachings have made a powerful impact in my walk with our Lord Jesus Christ. I look forward to learning from you again.

Pastor Akila Alles, was the first person I met, on my first day at a Christian theological seminary. From what I know, you have a very busy schedule with work, church, and ministry. Yet on that night you picked up my random call and prayed boldly. Your prayers edified me. I believe you were a divine connection, by God for His purpose. Pastor Akila, thank you for reaching out.

Pastor Rajah Solomon and **Tanuja Rajah,** stood by me, as I braved my way to do Christian art and word exhibitions in Sri Lanka, many years ago. I was an awarded artist in school but was a hopeless writer. Pastor Rajah, opened my eyes to write about practical Christianity. He said, *"You will write books"*. Four years later, the first book was published. Thank you for standing with me in the gap, throughout the years. Thank you for praying for me with your intercessory prayer team.

Amma (Mother) enthusiastically listened to the first draft of the manuscript being read out and corrected my grammar (big grin). Amma, it was very painful to see you suffer through hip surgery and the road to recovery. I love you. Lord Jesus Christ loves you more. It is my hope, you will meet my Lord, my Savior, and my Redeemer.

Kesara graciously photographed my art and art exhibitions with his team, many years back. I joyfully use these images in my publishing, marketing, promotional, and commercial endeavors. Thank you, my friend.

Nuzaifa graciously read the manuscript and pointed out areas of edits. Where were those words (big grin), I wonder? You have shown that it is necessary to have a fresh set of eyes read through the mass of words. Thank you for your kind words of appreciating the career mentorship, many moons back. Thank you for encouraging me to keep mentoring. Thank you, my friend.

My dearest nephew **Savi,** what a wonderful man you have grown to be. I thank God for giving you a heart of service. You are truly blessed and favored, time will reveal you, in the true light, you are meant to shine. Thank you!

Mariza what a wonderful listener you have become. Thank you for listening to me for hours at the end, especially when my mother was in hospital. Thank you for your love and friendship.

Thank you to the network of prayer intercessors. A special thank you goes to Nimmi, Therese, and Sarla. Thanking God for His mighty intercessors.

Thank you, team **WestBow Press**, for a joyful and peaceful publishing journey. Book two done. Praise God!

BIBLIOGRAPHY

All scriptures are quoted from https://www.biblegateway.com/

MOUNT CARMEL PROPHET CHALLENGE
https://www.biblegateway.com/passage/?search=1+Kings+17&version=NLT
https://www.biblegateway.com/quicksearch/?quicksearch=Mount+Carmel+Prophet&version=NLT
https://www.biblegateway.com/passage/?search=1+Kings+18&version=NLT

ELIJAH RAN IN FEAR
https://www.biblegateway.com/passage/?search=1+Kings+19&version=NLT

I OPENED A DOOR FOR FEAR
https://www.biblegateway.com/quicksearch/?quicksearch=fourth+generation+&version=NKJV
https://www.biblegateway.com/quicksearch/?quicksearch=Christ%2Bredeemed&version=NKJV
https://www.biblegateway.com/quicksearch/?quicksearch=power+over+the+enemy&version=NKJV

ONSLAUGHT ON THE MIND
https://www.biblegateway.com/quicksearch/?quicksearch=grace+is+sufficient&version=NLT
https://www.biblegateway.com/quicksearch/?quicksearch=Spiritual+battle&version=NLT

I RAN IN FEAR
https://www.biblegateway.com/passage/?search=Isaiah+54%3A17&version=NKJV

A VERY STRANGE VISIT
https://www.biblegateway.com/quicksearch/?quicksearch=discerning+spirits&version=NKJV
https://www.biblegateway.com/passage/?search=2+Timothy+2%3A22&version=NLT

THE HOLY SPIRIT TAKES OVER
https://www.biblegateway.com/quicksearch/?quicksearch=God+has+not+given+us+a+spirit+of+fear&version=NLT
https://www.biblegateway.com/quicksearch/?qs_version=NLT&quicksearch=Love+of+God&startnumber=51

PRAYER AND WORSHIP MARATHON
https://www.biblegateway.com/quicksearch/?quicksearch=Philadelphia&version=NLT
https://www.biblegateway.com/quicksearch/?quicksearch=victory%2Bbanner&version=NLT

https://www.biblegateway.com/quicksearch/?quicksearch=David%2Bcave&version=NLT
https://www.biblegateway.com/quicksearch/?quicksearch=dancing&version=NLT
https://www.biblegateway.com/quicksearch/?quicksearch=Holy+Spirit+%2B+remind&version=NLT
https://www.biblegateway.com/passage/?search=Revelations+3%3A7&version=NLT
https://www.biblegateway.com/quicksearch/?quicksearch=David%2Bcave%2Bprayer&version=NLT
https://www.biblegateway.com/passage/?search=Psalm+142&version=NLT
https://www.biblegateway.com/quicksearch/?quicksearch=dancing&version=NLT
https://www.biblegateway.com/quicksearch/?quicksearch=Miriam+&version=NLT
https://www.biblegateway.com/passage/?search=Exodus+15&version=NLT

OVERCOMER'S CHECKLIST

https://www.biblegateway.com/quicksearch/?quicksearch=guard+your+heart&version=NLT
https://www.biblegateway.com/passage/?search=Isaiah+60%3A1&version=NLT
https://www.biblegateway.com/quicksearch/?quicksearch=Lord%2B+fight+for+you&version=NLT
https://www.biblegateway.com/quicksearch/?quicksearch=Imitate+Christ&version=NLT
https://www.biblegateway.com/quicksearch/?quicksearch=False+prophets&version=NLT
https://www.biblegateway.com/passage/?search=Jeremiah+23&version=NLT
https://www.biblegateway.com/quicksearch/?qs_version=NLT&quicksearch=thoughts&startnumber=26
https://www.biblegateway.com/passage/?search=Ephesians%204&version=NLT
https://www.biblegateway.com/passage/?search=Matthew+15&version=NKJV
https://www.biblegateway.com/quicksearch/?quicksearch=think+%2B++spirit&version=NLT
https://www.biblegateway.com/quicksearch/?quicksearch=love+your+enemy+&version=NKJV
https://www.biblegateway.com/quicksearch/?quicksearch=Christ+forgave+you&version=NKJV
https://www.biblegateway.com/passage/?search=James+4+&version=NKJV
https://www.biblegateway.com/quicksearch/?quicksearch=All+things+work+for+good&version=NLT

WORDS OF ENCOURAGEMENT

https://www.biblegateway.com/quicksearch/?quicksearch=Publish+&version=NLT

INTERCESSORY PRAYER

https://www.biblegateway.com/quicksearch/?quicksearch=Pray%2Ball+people&version=NLT

A PRISONER WAS SET FREE
https://www.biblegateway.com/quicksearch/?quicksearch=Angel%2BPeter&version=NLT
https://www.biblegateway.com/passage/?search=Acts%2012&version=NLT
https://www.biblegateway.com/quicksearch/?quicksearch=Faith%2BGod%2Bplease&version=NLT
https://www.biblegateway.com/quicksearch/?quicksearch=Spiritual%2Bfoolish&version=NLT

WORSHIP LED BY THE HOLY SPIRIT!
https://www.biblegateway.com/quicksearch/?quicksearch=spirit+and+truth&version=NKJV
https://www.biblegateway.com/quicksearch/?quicksearch=please%2Bspirit&version=NLT
https://www.biblegateway.com/quicksearch/?quicksearch=spirit%2Bthoughts&version=NLT
https://www.biblegateway.com/quicksearch/?quicksearch=sons+of+God%2BSpirit&version=NKJV
https://www.biblegateway.com/quicksearch/?quicksearch=new+creation+&version=NKJV
https://www.biblegateway.com/quicksearch/?quicksearch=communion&version=NKJV

PRISONERS WERE SET FREE
https://www.biblegateway.com/quicksearch/?quicksearch=Paul%2BSilas%2BPrison&version=NKJV
https://www.biblegateway.com/passage/?search=Acts%2016&version=NKJV
https://www.biblegateway.com/quicksearch/?qs_version=NLT&quicksearch=Holy+Spirit&startnumber=26
https://www.biblegateway.com/quicksearch/?quicksearch=deep+things%2BGod&version=NLT
https://www.biblegateway.com/quicksearch/?quicksearch=Holy+Spirit%2Bteaches&version=NLT
https://www.biblegateway.com/quicksearch/?quicksearch=Spirit%2Bspeak&version=NLT
https://www.biblegateway.com/quicksearch/?quicksearch=true+worship&version=NLT
https://www.biblegateway.com/quicksearch/?quicksearch=Sing+praises+to+the+Lord&version=NLT

FIGHT WITH WORDS
https://www.biblegateway.com/quicksearch/?qs_version=NLT&quicksearch=power+of+God&startnumber=76
https://www.biblegateway.com/quicksearch/?quicksearch=Holy+Spirit%2Bgroaning&version=NLT
https://www.biblegateway.com/quicksearch/?quicksearch=speaking+in+tongues&version=NLT

https://www.biblegateway.com/passage/?search=1%20Corinthians%2014&version=NLT
https://www.biblegateway.com/quicksearch/?quicksearch=gift+of+the+spirit&version=NLT
https://www.biblegateway.com/quicksearch/?quicksearch=be+strong+and+courageous
&version=NLT
https://www.biblegateway.com/passage/?search=2+Timothy+1%3A7&version=NKJV
https://www.biblegateway.com/quicksearch/?quicksearch=Holy+Spirit%2Bhelp&
version=NKJV
https://www.biblegateway.com/quicksearch/?qs_version=NLT&quicksearch=+Love+of+
God&startnumber=51
https://www.biblegateway.com/quicksearch/?quicksearch=perfect+love&version=NLT
https://www.biblegateway.com/quicksearch/?quicksearch=mind+of+Christ&version=NLT
https://www.biblegateway.com/passage/?search=Isaiah+41%3A10&version=NLT
https://www.biblegateway.com/quicksearch/?quicksearch=renew+thoughts&version=NLT
https://www.biblegateway.com/quicksearch/?quicksearch=Holy+Spirit+power&
version=NLT
https://www.biblegateway.com/quicksearch/?quicksearch=Holy+Spirit%2Bpreach&
version=NLT
https://www.biblegateway.com/passage/?search=1%20Corinthians%2012&version=NLT
https://www.biblegateway.com/quicksearch/?quicksearch=fight+%2Bbattles&version=NLT
https://www.biblegateway.com/quicksearch/?quicksearch=Prophesies%2Bencourages&
version=NLT

JOURNEY CONTINUES
https://www.biblegateway.com/quicksearch/?quicksearch=fruit+of+the+spirit&version=NLT
https://www.biblegateway.com/quicksearch/?quicksearch=Jesus%2Bstorm&version=NLT
https://www.biblegateway.com/passage/?search=Matthew%208&version=NLT
https://www.biblegateway.com/passage/?search=Isaiah+60%3A1-2&version=NLT
https://www.biblegateway.com/passage/?search=Romans+12&version=NLT

BRAND NEW YOU IN CHRIST, art and words
Published by WestBow Press

BRAND NEW YOU IN CHRIST, urges a Christian to embrace, grow, and move forward in the brand new identity in Christ Jesus in the marketplace. A brand identifies with its maker in the marketplace. Likewise, a Christian's life must identify with its maker - Lord Jesus Christ. Don't worry if you do not see immediate result of becoming a born again Christian. We don't see what is happening to the caterpillar inside the cocoon. We see the end result of the butterfly. Just as a caterpillar becomes a butterfly, a believer's life is changed by the Holy Spirit to reveal something brand new!

JOURNEY OF FAITH: RESPONDING TO GOD'S CALLING TESTIMONY IN ART AND WORDS can be viewed via the following link https://web.facebook.com/photo/?fbid=587985120008667& set=pcb.587861643354348

Printed in the United States
by Baker & Taylor Publisher Services